Songs of Horses and Lovers

Songs of Horses and Lovers

Poetry by Madelyne Camrud

[signature] Madelyne Camrud
March 1– 2018

North Dakota State University Press
Dept. 2360, P.O. Box 6050, Fargo, ND 58108-6050
www.ndsupress.org

North Dakota State University Press
Dept. 2360, P.O. Box 6050, Fargo, ND 58108-6050
www.ndsupress.org

Songs of Horses and Lovers
Poetry by Madelyne Camrud

©2018 by North Dakota State University Press
First Edition

ISBN: 978-0-911042-99-3
Library of Congress Control Number: 2017954604

Original art by Madelyne Camrud
Photographs in possession of author
Cover design by Jamie Hohnadel Trosen
Interior design by Deb Tanner
Digital reproductions of artwork by Jason Restemayer
Editorial interns: Angela Beaton, Samuel Caspers, Shane Gomes, Zachary Vietz

The publication of *Songs of Horses and Lovers* is made possible by the generous support of donors to the NDSU Press Fund and the NDSU Press Endowment Fund.

For copyright permission, please contact Suzzanne Kelley at 701-231-6848 or suzzanne.kelley@ndsu.edu

Printed in Canada

Publisher's Cataloging-In-Publication Data
(Prepared by The Donohue Group, Inc.)

Names: Camrud, Madelyn Roeder.
Title: Songs of horses and lovers : poetry / by Madelyne Camrud.
Description: First edition. | [Fargo, North Dakota] : North Dakota State University Press, [2018]
Identifiers: ISBN 978-0-911042-99-3
Subjects: LCSH: Camrud, Madelyn Roeder--Family--Poetry. | Women--North Dakota--Poetry. | Norwegian Americans--North Dakota--Poetry. | Frontier and pioneer life--North Dakota--Poetry.
Classification: LCC PS3553.A4887 S66 2018 | DDC 811/.54--dc23

∞ This paper meets the requirements of ANSI/NISO Z39.48-1992 (Permanence of Paper).

*This book of songs
is dedicated to the memories of
my maternal grandmother, Mali, and my mother, Martine.*

I sing for all sisters and daughters.

I hate the coast; it means the end of land.
—Meridel le Suer

*The boundless vista and the horizon far and dim are all here;
And this is ocean's poem.*
—Walt Whitman, "In Cabin'd Ships at Sea," *Leaves of Grass*

ix   Acknowledgements
1   Prelude

First
Mali (1872–1966)

5   Mother of my mother,
7   Mother of water,
13   Grief, a weight
17   Down the road, love
21   Every year she grew smaller,
25   Mother of snow,

29   **Second**
Martine (1908–1999)

31   After a long night,
32   Close by on the beach,
39   Olaus, Olaus, how like a song
41   Hired, a girl of fifteen
42   Cousin Hilda married
44   Two sisters down the road,
45   Mother, I am sorry

47   **Third**
Milton and Martine (1928–1965)

49   The wedding was small,
55   He cracked the reins
57   See them driving,
59   Mother steps onto a rock,
64   She worked like a horse,
65   I want to tell you

71   **Fourth**
Prairie Hymn (2000–   )

75   Mother of water,
82   Mother, at last
84   I ride to the river,
86   I go back
87   Mother wanders
88   Roses spring up
90   I take the voice of my father
92   In last night's dream,
95   Horse, oh horse,

97   Postlude

Glossary

Acknowledgements

"Close by on the beach," chosen a finalist in *The Ledge* 1996 Poetry Competition, first appeared in *The Ledge*, spring 1997.

"Mother of water," (shortened version) appeared in *On Second Thought: A Publication of the North Dakota Humanities Council*, September 2016.

First thanks go to my mother, Martine, "proud to be 100 percent Norwegian." Her love of language—Norwegian and English, along with her stories were my inspiration for this collection. I thank Jay Meek for his advice when I began graduate studies: "Why not study Norwegian when you have a mother who can advise you?" Thanks to my sister, Jeannette Klevberg, who appealed to aunts, friends, and cousins for details that fleshed out the stories Mother told us, and for my one remaining sister, Carla, for her love of family history about which we are still privileged to converse. Ultimately, I thank David Mason for a semester of work at Minnesota State University Moorhead. Our time together the fall of '97 was essential in shaping *Songs of Horses and Lovers* into a publishable collection.

Thanks to North Dakota State University Press, especially Suzzanne Kelley, Editor in Chief, who encouraged me to submit *Songs*, and to the Press's editorial interns and reviewers for their attention to the work. I thank Melissa Gjellstad, Associate Professor of Languages, University of North Dakota, and Faythe Thureen, my Norwegian instructor in the 1980s at UND; these women were essential for the glossary. Thanks to Lenore Anderson for the Family Group Sheets; to art photographer, Jason Restemayer, and for the author photo, Jodi M. Smith. Special thanks to Barbara Crow and other early readers who insisted the "Songs" were worth saving. All these years later, I remain grateful for everyone who helped bring this collection to completion, especially my late husband, Ted, and my family who always understood, accepted, and supported my need to create.

Prelude

In that valley below Meråker,
the purple twilight that stayed long past midnight,
Grandmother came to me in a dream, her face sifting like snow
onto a gray board. She stood at the gate,
her birthplace,
and invited me inside.

The First

Mali (1872–1966)

Like echoes, the women last longer;
                      they're all too tough for their own good.

                                      —Louise Gluck

Mother of my mother,

    Break that mountain like *fossen* gushing; leave the goats and *kuer*, *ost* and *smør*;
                  leave the *seter*. Rush through birch trees

    and evergreens, flow from grass and pine; carve your name again in the trunk
                  that holds your life, paint it with roses

    that trailed your mother's gate. Leave your mother, vines on the fence where
                  she stood waving the day of your passage;

    leave your father, sisters, brothers; leave that small house, rooms you swept
                  with pine bough broom; leave the rocks,

    the *sur jord*, and board the train north from *Flornes*; leave *Sonfossen, nedre, vestre* —
                  leave again the land you left, the lack it means.

    Join that long stream of women rushing into the North Sea, flowing into that ocean
                  deep, green and cold.

*Somewhere in the gray-green water
between Trondheim
and Bergen, riding the* Hurtigruta
*on that wild,
tormented sea, I lost all desire
for home and order.*

Mother of water,

    I hear you drumming in the belly of that steamer, bobbing over like a note sent
        in a bottle; seasick, heaving up,

    down, coming up for air to live. Begin the dancing now, the strumming, shoes
        thumping the salty planks, arms

    pumping up and down, red-bearded uncle your partner, dancing as if your life
        depended on rhythm, steam driven,

    wooden deck. Eating dried fish, moldy bread, white cheese and yellow, I hunger
        with you for milk and potatoes.

    Mother of water, I am calling; answer me in language broken, but sure; find me
        in the dank stench of that galley

    filled with wooden kegs and trunks; hear me on that trek of sky and water,
        admirers passing, turning their heads,

eyes feasting on you not quite five feet in high shoes, waist nipped, cotton to bone.
Trønder woman from close to *Lapland*,

saucy cheekbones high and stern, jaw lifted to face the wind, let me catch with you
the sea's flavor, salt of the ocean

on our tongues; let me love you for your daring, rocked to distant shores, beginning
in a new country. Let me ride with you,

east to Midwest, long rail to the valley, *posten*: Reynolds, North Dakota, muddy streets,
boardwalks, *lutefisk* in wooden barrels,

ambitious men.

For love,

       Mali found Olaus, both hired to work for the uncle. Two-day wedding: vows
                 in the schoolhouse, dancing the schottische

and polka, uncle's farm, eating *kjøttballer*, *potetklubb* until she let her hair down,
               and fell warm into the arms of Olaus.

       He bought a quarter-section for twelve hundred in the spring; and together they crossed
               the threshold of that small house,

the green earth ripening; water flowed like hope for a better life: cows to milk, pails
               to carry, cream to churn. Earth turned,

plowed deep; Mali and Olaus a team: horses harnessed, hog throats slashed for meat;
               chickens axed, feathers picked—

Mali cooked, baked, and cleaned. For love, she birthed nine children, chewed a wooden
               plug for pain, pulled a rag tied to the bedpost,

and pushed through blood and water until that day she pushed through mud, the slush
                of April, a black cloak draped over her shoulders.

She rode the carriage, horse-drawn, behind the hearse bearing Olaus. *Stjørdalen* church:
                stern-faced preacher led her and the mourners

black arm banded, a long line drawn down the aisle to that bald hill, the bell tolling
                until silent where they stood in cold wind,

stood where the stone still bears his name: Olaus Hjelmstad, a stone, stone-cold, stoney.

A widow that summer, she kept a calf
tied in the barn, fattened it
with extra milk for butchering, for winter meat.
One morning, went out to do the milking,
and found the calf still in its stall,
strangled in its own rope.

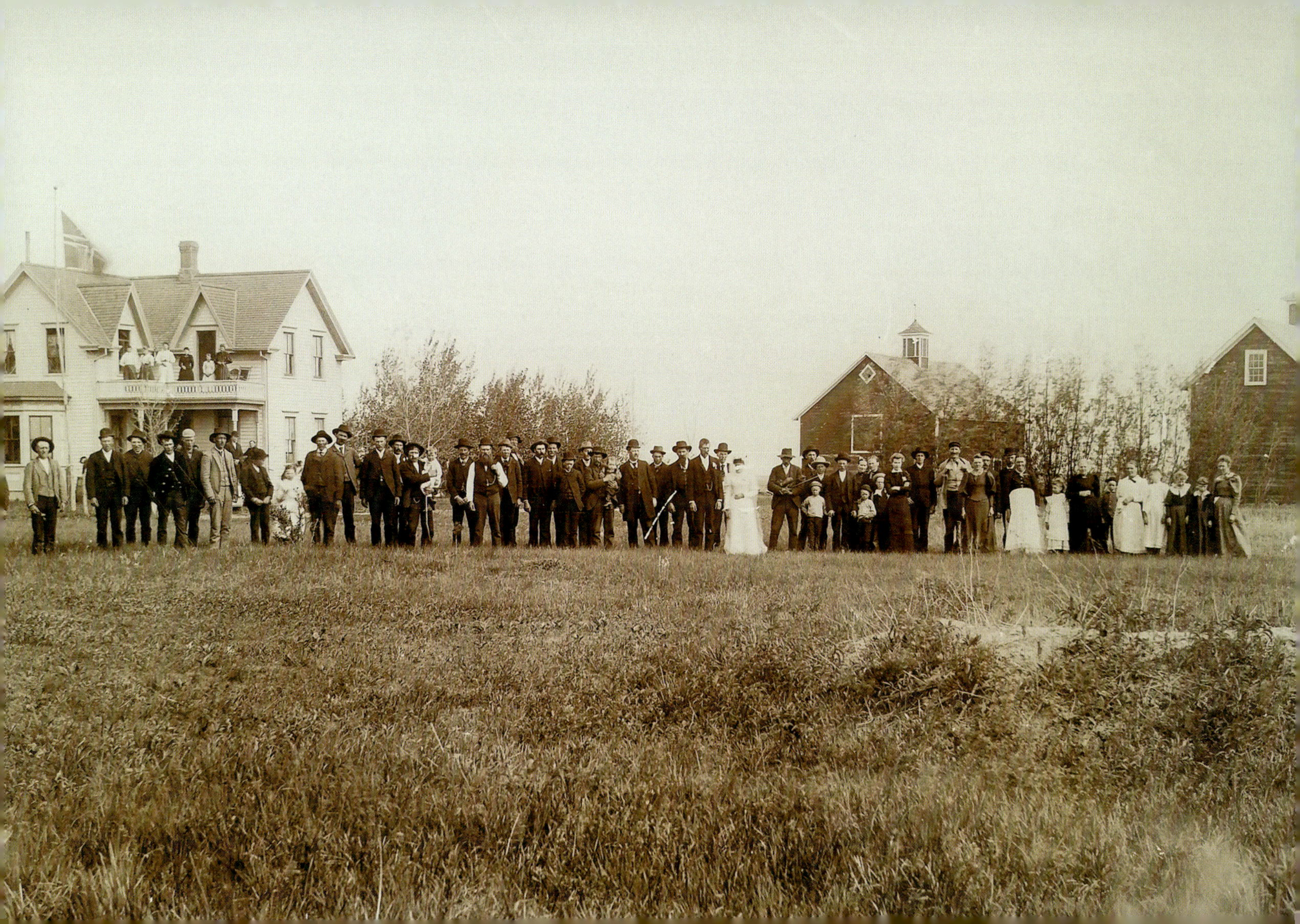

1. *Mali and Olaus, Wedding Reception (the Uncle's farm) Union Township, June 1894*
   Photograph
   8" X 11"

Grief, a weight

    on her shoulders every morning, one night washing dishes at the sink, her body
            shook. Small daughter asked, *Ma,*

    why are you laughing? Not laughing, Mali answered, *crying*. Oldest boys, twelve,
            another younger, mired down in mud-holes,

    tried to seed grain that spring. Planted potatoes, hoped for some to eat by July.
            Too hot, then dry, rain came, wrong time. Too few

    blooms couldn't produce. Oldest daughter seeded carrots, peas, and beans; forgot
            to thin them, none grew large enough to eat.

    Jeg leva i håpet som katta i skapet, was Mali's mantra. Daughter did better with flowers,
            moss roses for Mali, nasturtiums for the daughter.

    But the *hund* dug up the flowers, down to the roots, cool place to rest. Mali raised
            a stick to keep the boys from fighting,

but near the end of August when she turned forty-one, nights came on more quickly,
and, frost predicted, she made her decision.

Snow coming soon that November, she married Johannes, only way she knew to make
a living. He, a widower two years, more

than twenty her senior, fathered her last baby. Number ten lived but a week, died
from cramps. Her new husband built the casket,

Mali laid the baby inside, dressed in white, the cap and romper she knit.

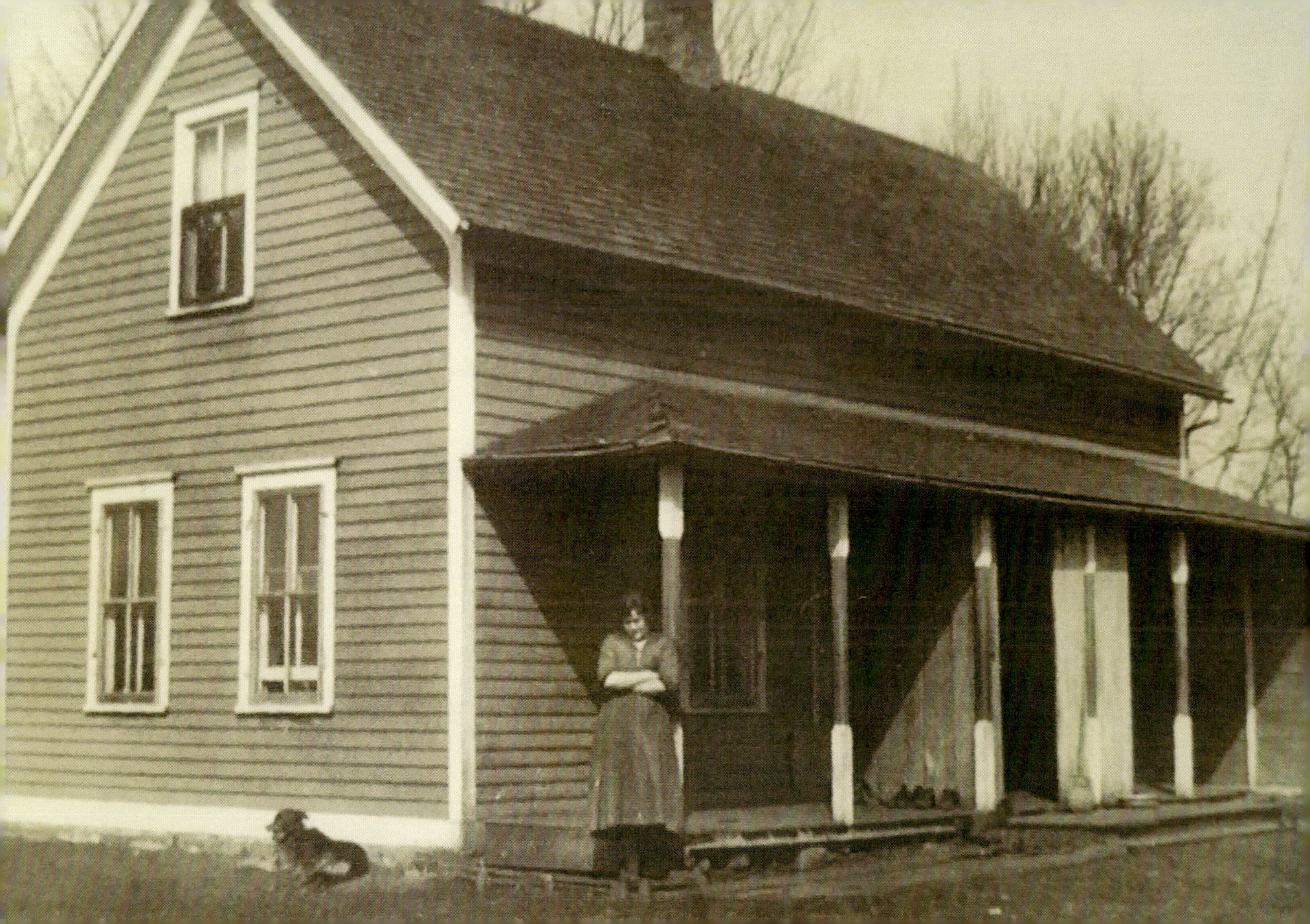

2. *Mali at Home with Johannes, 1914, Union Township*
   Snapshot
   3" X 5"

Down the road, love unspoken bound the neighbor girl to her brother; with him
       she bore a blind son.

The child sat all day in a chair; couldn't play with the others but he could sing
       and he did as he sat alone

in the kitchen; bones, blood in perfect measure; he, a single note in the world,
       no chance for a chord—

but a song, yes, a song—his voice his own where he sat by the window, cold draft;
       died from pneumonia when he was six.

And in my memory all I see is that neighbor's kitchen ceiling painted deep red.
       For all of us, time changes the color of the picture.

Black to red, a story told, comes back in songs for daughters. Sisters pretty,
                drew men like flies to honey:

daughters gazed at the moon; sisters played and sang in corn fields, fell like stars
                into darkness, danced with men

whose golden guitars played songs sweet as cream, the Milky Way. Men hired
                tilled the land, reined horses into harness;

men took the earth and worked it, smelled the sweet hay as calloused hands
                pitched forkfuls into stacks; the sweat

of their flesh gleamed in hot sun. Women brought lunch, buns with meat, water
                for the men; drank with pleasure the women

                who fed their hunger.

Daughters' skirts down or up, were watched by fathers. Some fell in love with sons
                         of neighbors the father hated, forbid

the daughters to see their lovers. One sent pregnant down the road, suitcase in hand.
                         Father blamed the hired man, claimed

he'd heard tell-tale strange noises in the haymow. How strange when the daughter
                         returned home to have the baby,

it was the father who sewed the diapers, made the layette. Later, the daughter
                         in spite of her father, chose to

marry the man her father hated (would have hated any one of them, they say).
                         The couple went away, spoke vows,

then came home to take the baby. The father hid that baby girl, tucked her with
                         him under the bridge, *No, no, you can't take her*.

         Fathers, daughters,

                         daughters, fathers.

Oh, the pricks, the pulls, the strange hold love can take—whatever holds a woman
                like the hoof-beat of a horse,

that rider-less shape waiting. Let this month's moon be the moon that wakes me,
                let it remove the shadow that covers me

like an ocean over the land. Let the moon, moving in and out like the tide
                washes the beach, wash me, the stories;

                let the words spoken and written wash us clean.

She had a black horse
named Florrie, white star on her forehead.
Too old to sell at auction,
they dug a hole in the pasture;
stood her beside it,
and shot her.

Every year she grew smaller, seated on that stool as if bent by a north wind,
gray hair drawn into a bun,

black shoes buttoned at her ankles. I never once heard her hum, but I sensed
a song inside her, through lips

pressed tightly shut; there was the slightest hint of strumming in her chest,
arms crossed under her breast.

I imagined songs from years of filling the pantry; cool, yellow shades that stored
the *lefse*, cold meatballs, milk soup

dumplings shaped perfectly as stitches taken to make her apron, dotted-Swiss;
                                  she was as neat as small pins

that stretched her lace curtains, pulled them tight on wooden racks. Once,
                                  she offered me sugar lumps;

another time, she asked to hold my first born son. Mali, like a small note
                                  grew into a letter, pages like those

sent from her mother, sisters, brother who wrote rhymes about their mother
                                  in Norway, how she whispered

from her grave for her daughter in Dakota, asked that he sing a greeting: the poem
                                  we found in Mali's trunk long after

she died, after she flew back and lit that mossy mountain, brook streaming below.

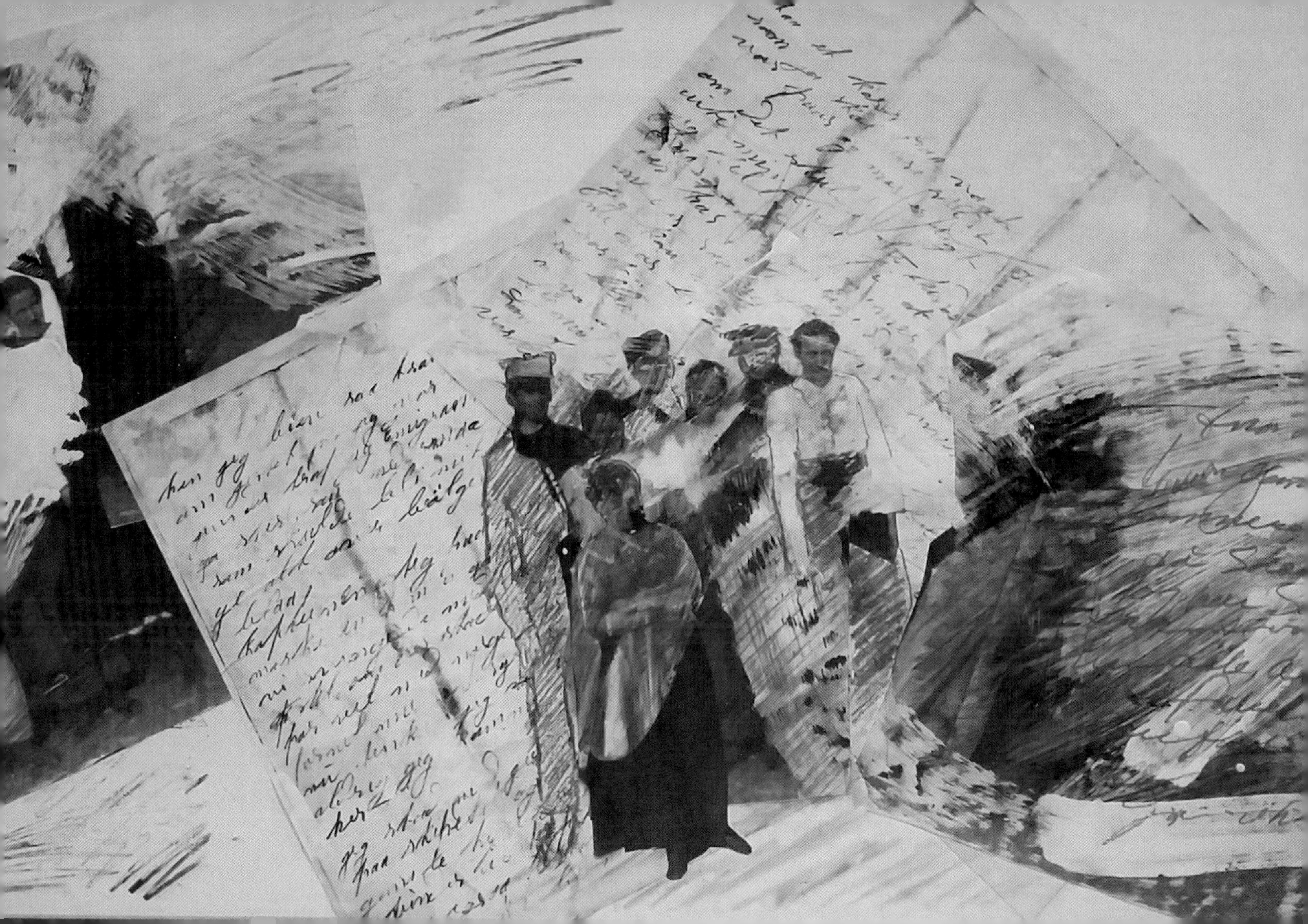

3. *Mali with Norwegian Cousins*
   Acrylic, charcoal, graphite, collaged letters from Norway on board
   12" X 22"

Mother of snow,

    first flakes driven by a strong wind, late October, I turn my head to the North—
            elixir of winter, time to go inside,

    time to find the heart's darkness: lovers lost, lovers found; women wailing
            in the cold, arms folded, holding

    their flesh to ease the pain. I find mine in the shape of your nose, your eyes, hair
            white as snow drawn tight, knot

    tied at the back of your head. Grandma Mali, I laid you out in wet snow as winter
            began; flakes shaped your profile

    washed color in what fell, looped your hair in curls that framed your face,
            carved you from memory

    the way a chisel breaks stone, makes art from granite.
            Mali, I crossed the ocean to find you.

*Somewhere in the gray-green water
I lost all desire for home and order.
Something in me like bodies cast over the side of boats,
wanted to taste forever the salt and vinegar
of the North Sea.*

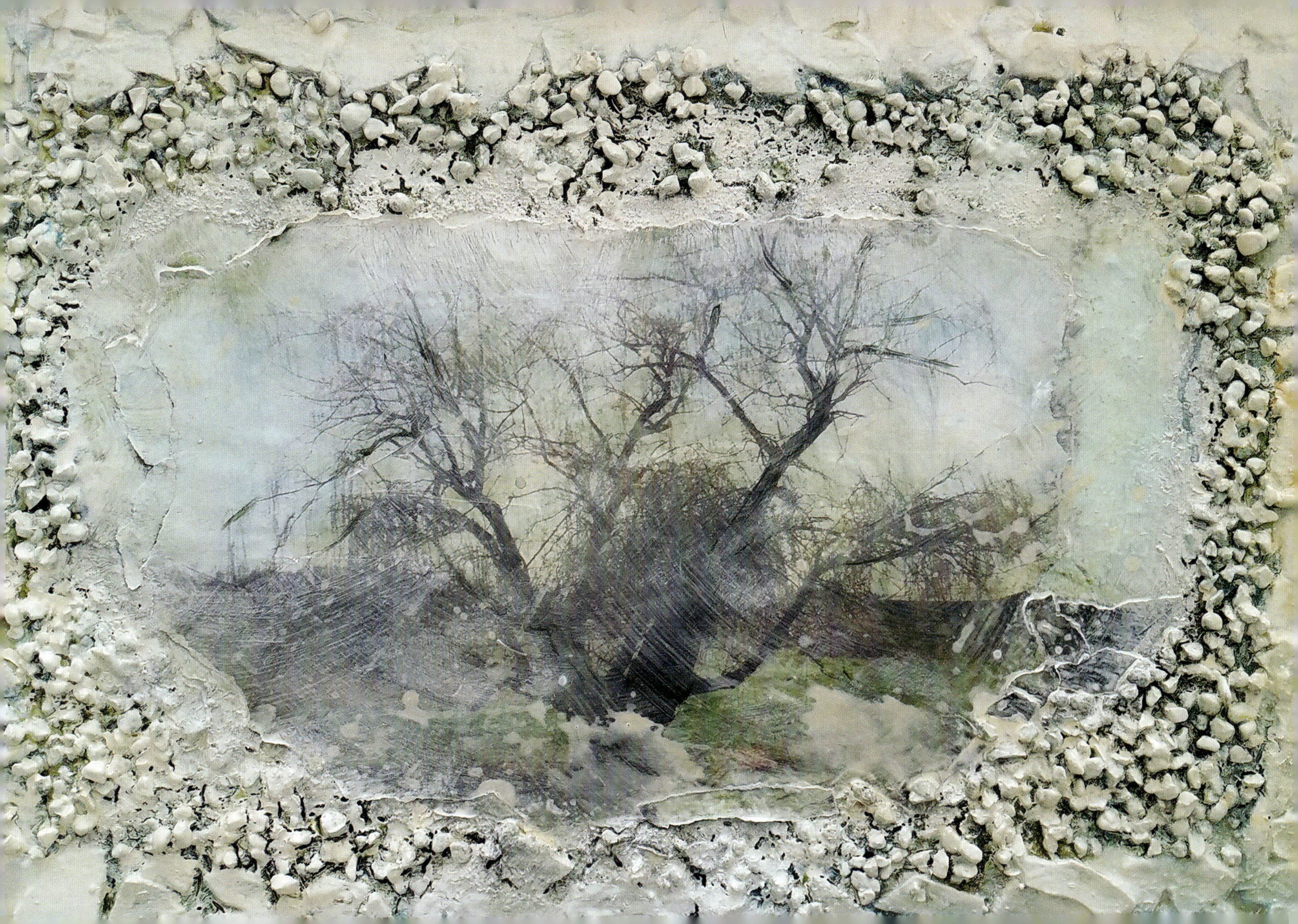

4. *The Family Tree (Weeping Willow)*
   Photograph with acrylic wash, mosaic mat of cracked marble and stone on board
   17" X 27"

The Second

Martine (1908–1999)

*What would happen if one woman told the truth about her life?
The world would split open* . . .

—Muriel Rukeyser

After a long night, I pull the veil of sleep from my face, waves on the beach
                no more than a flicker; I am nothing,

know nothing, dying must be like this: ships passing in the night, floating in fog,
                riding that gray endless space,

crossing waves, heading north. Like a leaf afloat, I'm carried where water spills
                from Mali's mountain. There,

grandmother's baby brother drowns in a stream, floats below the falls, face down.

                Mali named mother for him:

                Martine from Martin, *drukna i mølledam*,

                M-A-R-T-I-N-E.

Close by on the beach, in a patch of sapling popples, leaves dancing like coins,
                I catch scent of a horse

as if stopped by the shore after a long ride. I imagine sweat gleaming in rivulets
                down his flanks; muscles tense,

neck to forelocks, eyes still wild from the ride. But Mother, I cannot find him
                though my eyes sort the leaves;

all I have today is waves on the beach, names and stories, tales you told me of
                women and girls who broke the rules.

I recall your fleshy arms flopping as you worked, washing dishes, peeling potatoes.
                Told me one used a clothes hanger

for her abortion; another had her baby alone in the room upstairs, never daring
                to scream; she was the teacher,

one-room schoolhouse, her father such a Christian. She boarded at a farmhouse,
                walked to school each day.

One morning, the lady of the house called twice for breakfast and got no answer.
She knocked at the teacher's door,

opened it a crack, and a hand reached through, weak voice inside asked for water.
The lady pushed through the door,

found the baby, bloody and dead, laid in a shoebox.

Mother,

    I love your passion for words. How, on that morning, that dear teacher, her passion long since burned, must have

    longed for a horse to ride off on. But she stayed like the fetus in the box, its grim truth, stayed the way her body

    all that winter kept its secret, trudging that mile to the schoolhouse, facing cold wind, hard drifts, watching the seed

    that was growing in her belly. How strange it must have been, planning lessons, answering students' questions, when

    her own were much larger, and the shame—oh yes, the shame, how it must have grown with her waistline, drove

    her black boots through the snow; the man who'd spent his lust, all that winter, kept secret. That dear teacher must have

wished she hadn't let him have his way; no way to hasten the daily walk in her
                long skirt, loose coat, and heavy boots;

all that winter, trudging that mile morning and evening, thoughts blinding her,
                finding her way like a horse in a blizzard.

And that night when the pains came, she must have drawn the sheets up, covered
                her mouth to wrap the screams,

held them close to her face. Oh, how the pain, the shame, that long night must
                have burned until that small life

forced its way through blood and water only to die in the morning, landlady taking
                it as if it were no more than waste.

Daughters, fathers.
                              Fathers, daughters.

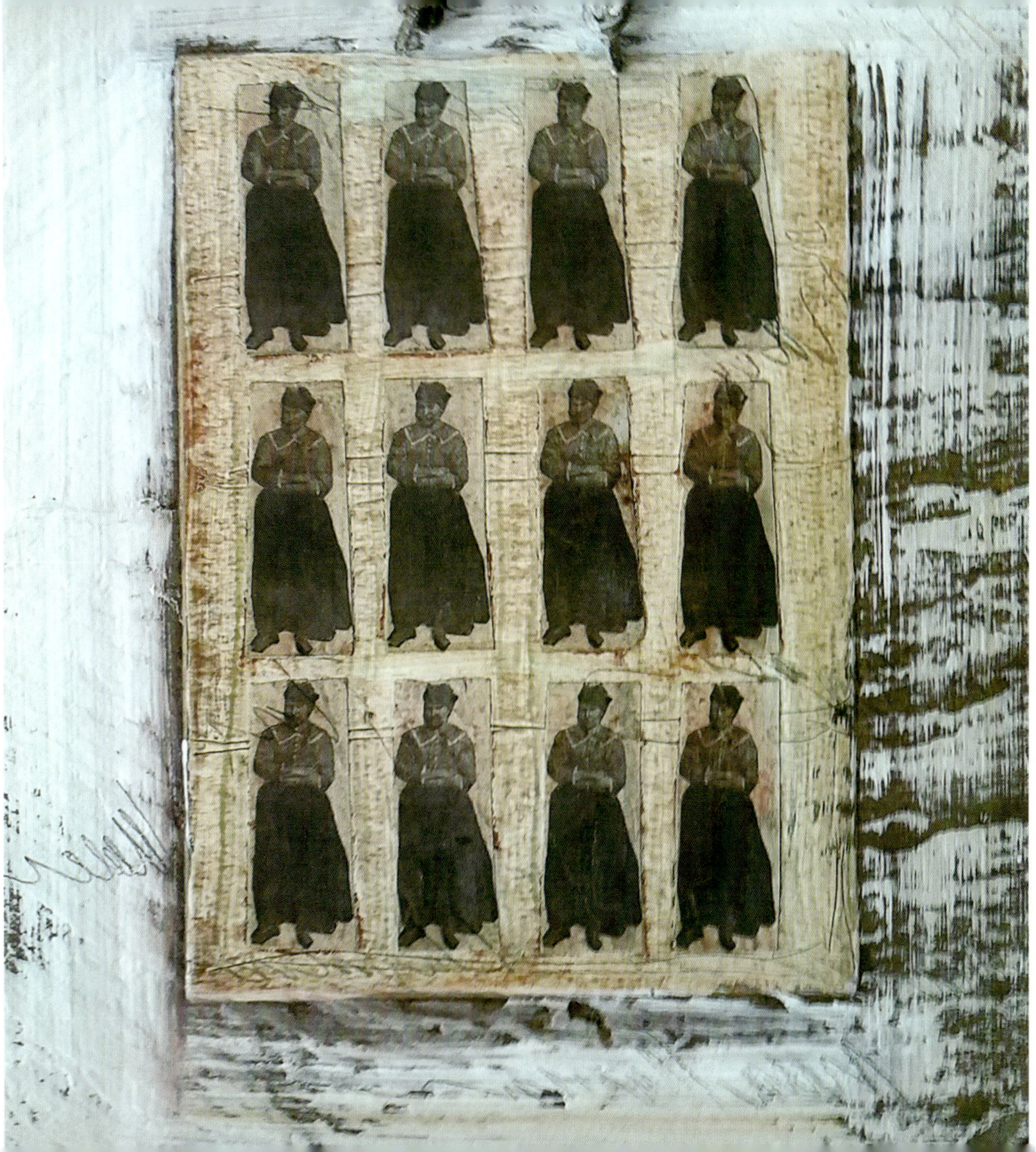

5. *Mali on Slate from Norway*
   Snapshot image, collage, acrylic
   24" X 10"

Olaus, Olaus,

    how like a song a name can be, sung over and over in a little girl's head.
            Told how you remember him

    lying on the couch, spitting the stuff from his lungs, tuberculosis spewed into
            the shiny brass spittoon.

    Sick all Christmas, heard him coughing all night through the bedroom walls.
            Gave you children silver dollars

    but in a game of toss yours landed in his sputum. Big brothers teased you,
            passed their fingers one over the other

    in shame and, by April, your father washed, laid out in the house, you tip-toed
            in and out, relatives coming, going,

    talking low until the wake ended, casket taken. The uncles ordered you from
            the room, children not knowing

the meaning of contagious, or fumigation. You stayed a moment, watched wicks
burning, long-tailed odor

filling the room, killing germs as if it were a way of saying: Father's gone for good
and no one should be sad; no little girl

should want to kiss him or wake him; should be quiet and follow the hearse
to the church where like a prince

he slept under glass; where someone lifted you, held you over the coffin:

Look as hard as you can, girl; you won't see him anymore.

Hired, a girl of fifteen to help a family of thirteen; the father, lecherous, pulled her
                onto his lap; pawed her breasts,

her hips, those precious parts full as fruit beginning to ripen. She scratched his hands
                until they bled, broke loose

from his grasp, and the wife watching, finally spoke: *You stupid fool! Now maybe*
                you'll leave the girl alone!

Each night before the girl slept, she dragged a dresser across the room and braced
                the closed door. Galloping, galloping

like the game played in school, she ran to the end of the field: *Pom, pom, pull away!*
                Don't let him catch you!

Four horses pulled the drill when brother Melvin,
age twelve, mired down in a mudhole.
She sat beside him for traction, but when
the neighbor came, told her she was
"*Too heavy,*" *he made her cry.*

Cousin Hilda married the man her father hated and, like a stone, he disowned her—
                    wouldn't speak to her, not even in church.

Bore one child after the other; weak after the fourth, lactating, she caught the flu
                    of 1918; it went to her brain.

Dying, she longed to make things right and called her father, *Please come. No, too cold*,
                    his answer. Hours passed until at last,

horses harnessed and hitched, he drove his sleigh through the snow, spent an hour
                    with his daughter, door closed. No one

knows what was said. All night, her brother wrote a song, the service, wrote all as if
                    the song might heal them, tune of

"Silver Threads among the Gold." She died next morning, the baby weeks old; in the worst
                    of winter, two days later, mourners

waited in the cold church, furnace out. Preacher's horses couldn't get through that snow,
                    cold winter any faster. The daughter

dressed in white like an angel in the casket, hair still dark, body young with soft curves.
                The preacher took her name in script,

pearl pin from her breast and pinned it on her baby, baptizing the child that day,
                the name given two ways: Hilda Hilda—

Mother, daughter, daughter, mother; sing with me now, dear Hilda, sing the way
                you sang, *Stjørdalen* church where no one

heard; sing today the way you sang over your baby: Funeral over, your father walked
                into the pew where your husband,

girl children sat, looked them over, *Spose I should take the baby but I'll take the older one,*
                she looks most like her mother.

        Your kind husband shook his head, *Sorry, you'll have none.*

Two sisters down the road shared a bed, worked as cooks, fed the hired men.
One morning, one sister rolled over,

let out a groan and had a baby, surprising her sister and everyone else.
When they asked, *who is the father?*

She asked back—*how do you know which teeth are cutting when you're
doing the sawing?*

Poison, poison . . . , don't touch me, game we used to play.

Run as fast as you can, girl, opposite direction of the one who dropped
a hanky at your ankles; find your place again
in the circle.

Mother,

        I am sorry for stories you wouldn't tell, stories like your bedroom door, varnished fir,
                  slammed shut. Stopped me

the way you stopped my sister's question: *how do I stop having babies?*
                Common sense, your answer,

common sense, that's all. And in the thickness of summer trees, too many leaves
                to see clearly, I hear your refrain:

So glad I had daughters; wouldn't know how to raise a son. Pregnant, I prayed
                each night, No sons, please.

                Four times God answered *Yes.*

*Her brothers hired her to lead the horse
to the trough for water, Moses, a bronco barely broke.
She tangled her foot in his rope
and fell; hoof grazed her face, came down on her ankle.
Her brothers laughed
and teased her. Moses went thirsty.*

Mother, when you asked: *Why do I have two bad daughters and two good ones?*

Knew where I stood then;
but I have come to love you for your stories, stories,
stories becoming songs.

The Third

Milton and Martine (1928–1966)

It is at the edge of the petal that love waits.

—William Carlos Williams

*Dad always said a man's success
should be measured by his horses.
Chose mother and his horses for two reasons:
good teeth and legs.*

The wedding was small, mother nervous, her dress beige crepe with a tinge of rose
                that matched her blush. She rode

to town with her brothers, met with the preacher, planned turkey dinner, German
                in-laws. He chose the best man,

her brother, and she, the maid-of-honor, her sister; a few others came for dinner;
                not her mother—she spoke only Norwegian.

End of the evening, the couple went to the movies, sat through twice before she
                let him take her home to that hotel room.

And, all the while the strong white horse beat his hooves, never quite coming through
                the snow, never through those thorny bushes

surrounding the moat. All the while, that bit of romance I remember: bouquet of
                roses stored in the chest lined with cedar,

dried for years, lace bow wrapping its thorny stems—the dress cut into bits, made into
                a quilt, long before I opened the lid,

caught no sweet aroma. In the photo, crepe falling over her breasts, fullness draped
                at her waist, they sit; father leaning close,

face chiseled like a rock, narrow nose, thick eyebrows; she, soft, round spectacled,
                finger-waved hair, holds the bouquet.

They sit, not quite smiling, as if knowing something left unsaid, something they
                knew between them I don't know.

Dad had five horses when they married,
all of them black: Dexter, Maud,
Tracy and Dan before Daisy. Took five to pull a gang;
three in front, two in back.

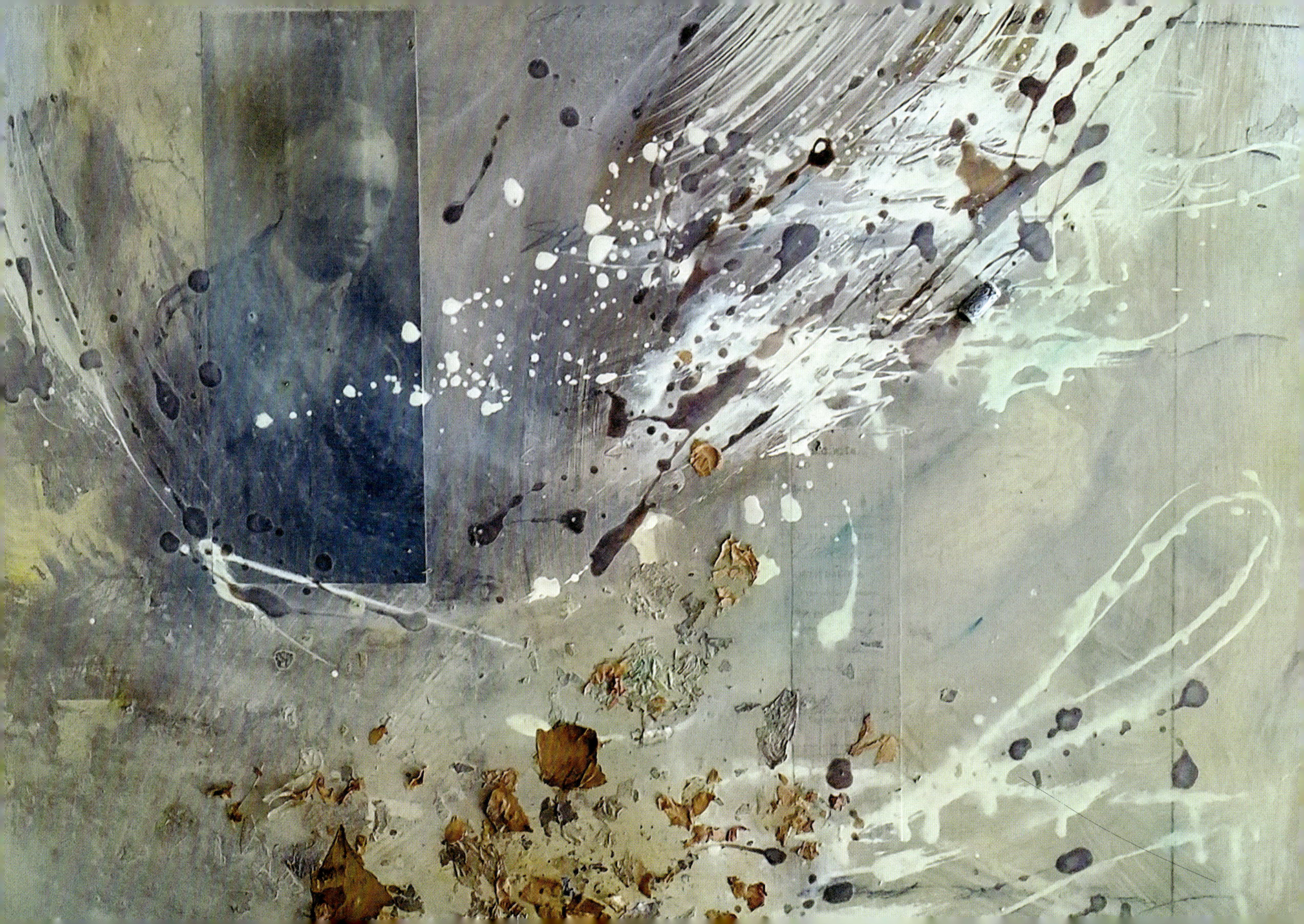

6. *In Memorium: Wedding Photograph, Dad's Half*
   Acrylic wash, paint, collage elements on board
   24" X 24"

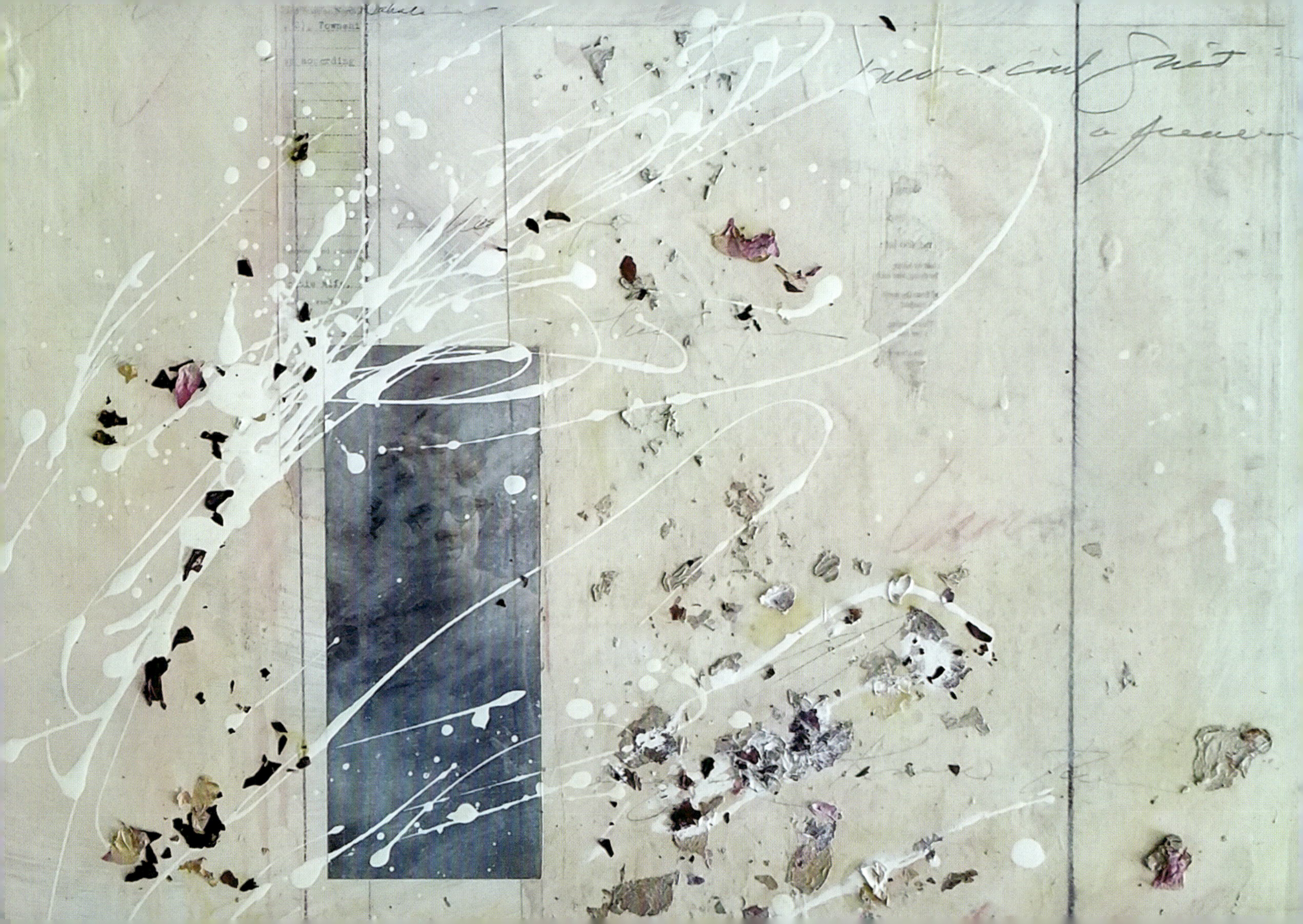

7. *In Memorium: Wedding Photograph, Mom's Half*
   Acrylic wash, paint, collage elements on board
   24" X 24"

He cracked the reins on their backsides, swore *Giddyyap* and *Whoa*, horseflesh
                        chosen for good reason.

Scolded her for walking with her head down; a hundred times she answered:
                        I am *Trønder*; the lowest class.

Shame kept her in harness like a horse on a bit, wearing blinders, washing the
                        underwear of men, two of them hired,

one hers; she boiled the whites of them in Hilex, spilled stories over the washer;
                        told how one girl caught her hair

in the wringer, pulled out a hunk with some scalp. I lived in fear of the wringer,
                        Mother's water turned grayer,

colder with each load, stories told over galvanized tubs for rinsing, stories of horses,
                        stories scrubbed, washed clean.

Last week,

    a sex offender interviewed on TV says he has no control over his strong
            sexual feelings, knows he'll rape again

like before when he killed a girl, fourteen. Now he walks the street in
            Stillwater, Minnesota, a free man.

           The hired girl, older, wiser, shouts,

                  CASTRATE HIM.

Dan and Daisy, a team again; one sorrel,
one chestnut, pulling the hayrack home from threshing;
clippity-clop, cloppity-clip,
black with crickets.

See them driving, Mother and Dad in the '41 Ford; the winter, blue and cold.
Mother in the fox coat

Dad trapped, sold fox pelts to buy. And I in long stockings, snow pants, cap,
and coat, stand on the hump

in the back, my blonde curls tossing, bouncing like waves leaping in and out
as we ride. Mother chatters;

Dad listens, making that funny sound he makes in his throat when contented.
We go humming along,

no thoughts of failures or successes in a landscape untouched, pre-missile base,
war only in newsreels

on the Reynolds town hall screen, gray faces flickering, voices floating over water
like ships afloat, those who

wanted to meet me halfway as we rode in the blue of the evening, the moon shining
clear and white like stone.

He bought a white horse named Byrd,
taken from the prairie; couldn't bring her to pull
a hayrack; at sight of a rope
she'd go crazy.

Mother steps onto a rock, snakes all around, nest of babies come out from under,
slithering in the grass, Mother

like Medusa, screaming, flesh turning cold. Ditches moist from spring run-off,
she'd been walking in ditches,

looking for turkey eggs, when she came upon this nest she hadn't expected.
Back at the farm, hens in the coop

cackled in the straw, scratching nests of their own. The cows, lazy as ever, graze
the pasture, calves on wobbly legs

close behind teats filled with milk; and the horses, serene, at a distance, stand
flicking their tails in brisk wind.

It's the kind of day that leads you from one thing to another by scent, but not Mother.
She stands, locked in her housedress

and apron on a rock, snakes writhing all around, her hair drawn back with two
brown combs, mouth half-open, she holds

a scream, stone, stone, stone-cold,

the stoneboat.

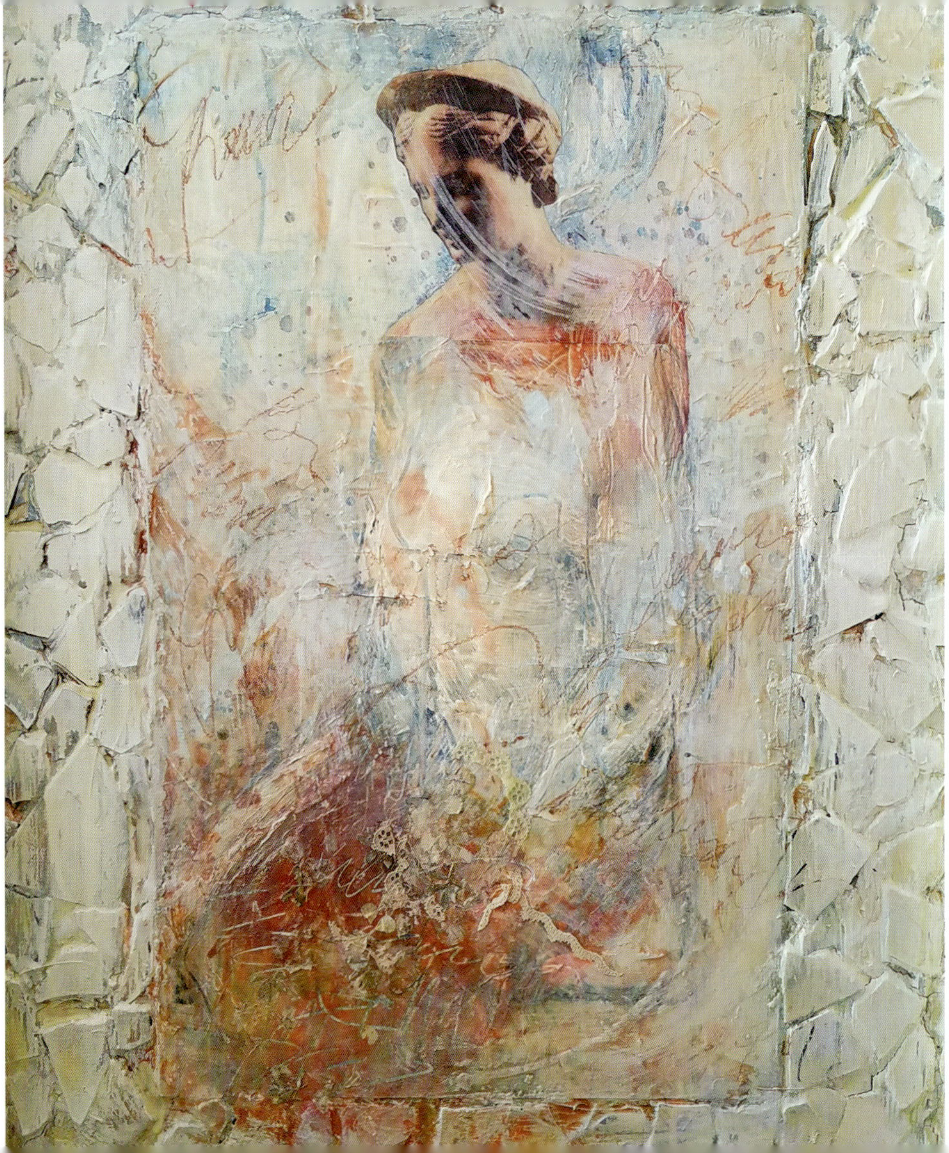

8. *Mother Forever*
   Acrylic with mosaic, collage on board
   33" X 22"

Dad comes through corn stubble. Shucks loaded on the stoneboat, he comes home
                from the fields; the cold moves in,

late autumn sunset. He stands at the front, holding Daisy by the reins as he hauls
                corn shucks into the orange sky, ablaze.

He could be Midas hauling gold, hauling the stuff of his life home for winter, hauling
                it home for animal fat, the heat of animals,

his woman, survival until summer. He's coming home, serene in his stone-boat,
                riding that long horizon, horse to pull him,

              riding into the sky, stone-boat afloat,
                  on land so flat and sweet.

Four in the boat and the boat goes 'round
Four in the boat and the boat goes 'round,
Four in the boat and the boat goes 'round,
bring home the pretty one you have found.

She worked like a horse, grit her teeth as if bridled. She took the bit; she cooked
                        and baked, she did the barn-chores,

and washed the underwear of men: two hired, one hers: *Men, men*, the word resounded
                        in her head and now in mine,

the way she said it with distaste; how it became at times *those men*, as if by saying it
                        she threw them like overalls

into the washtub. Long tough winters, she spoke of men, only men come to visit,
                        neighbor women couldn't walk

that long driveway's deep snow. Oh, how she tired of seeing men, only men.
                        Men, men, men. Amen.

I want to tell you about a man, never in a word but always in my soul; the man
        who speaks in silence, who wanders

alone on the prairie; he rides a horse, he braves blizzards. I crossed the pasture,
        and at the edge of the coulee, waded

through cattails, cow-prints and crayfish, found him building a smudge for cattle,
        mosquitoes. Had not seen him for days,

when, home from the field, he came to meet me, his face covered with field-dirt,
        peeled back, he grinned, called my name,

voice high like a hawk-cry. We waded through that lush distance, crossed the purple
        of twilight as if we floated,

        nearly touching.

Today, like birds outside the window, he suddenly lights the hedge. I know him
                at sight of the blue jay flying in;

he listens with me for the screech owl in a tree near my house, his voice the quiet
                inside me. Sat on his warm lap

and he taught me to tie my shoes; ran to him after mother washed my hair; after
                I hid, afraid of pulled snarls, hid

behind the Home Comfort range. He's not the man they wheeled from our house that June
                morning, not the one they carried

down the steps, cart under a sheet. Not that shell hollowed out from cancer—
                not my father, he's the one I seek

at twilight, listen for on the prairie those first fresh days of spring, and again in
                the somber winter stillness. He's the one

who taught me to listen, to learn the music inside me but, Mother, you're the one
                who taught me to sing.

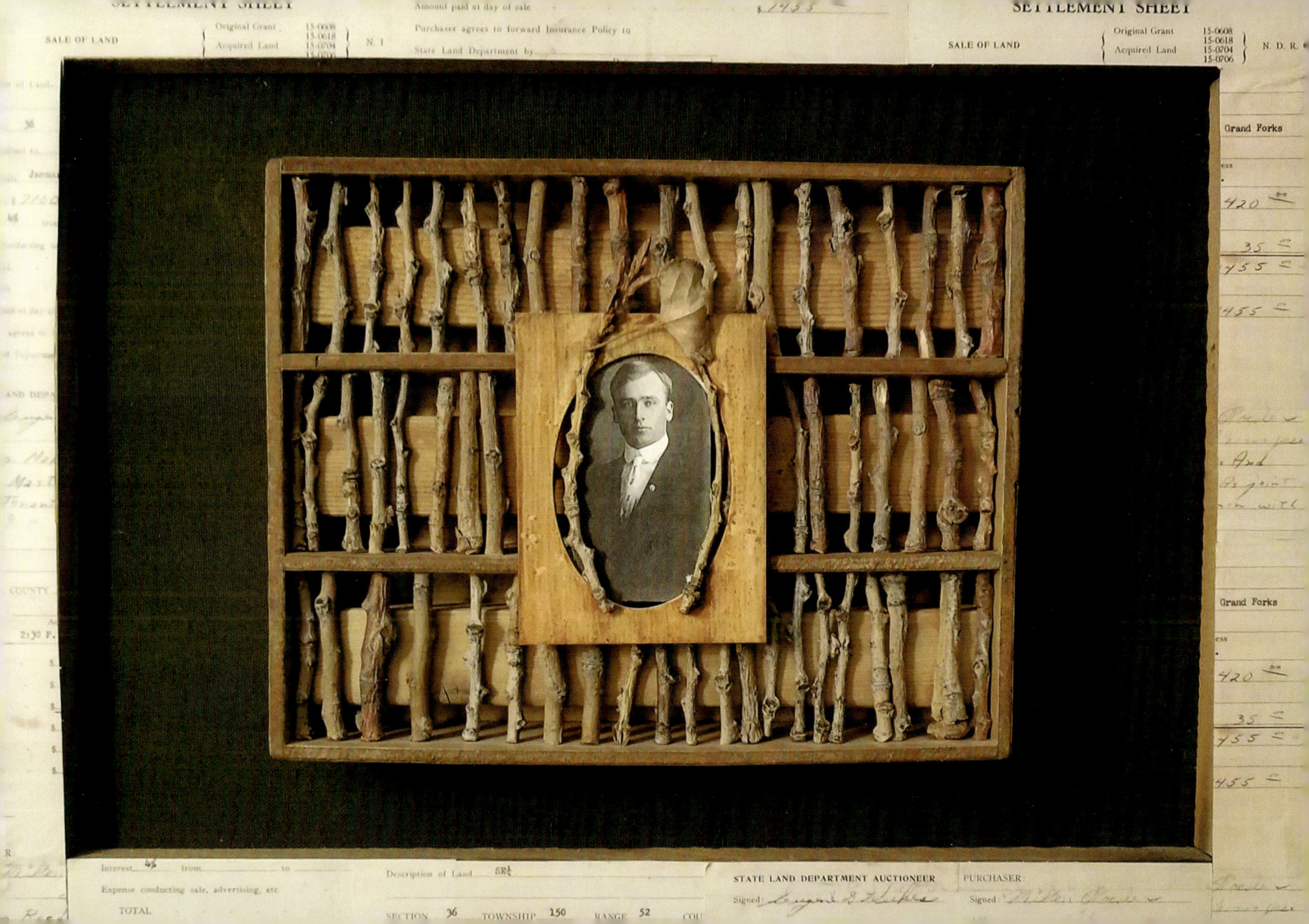
SETTLEMENT SHEET
SALE OF LAND
Original Grant
Acquired Land
15-0608
15-0618
15-0704
15-0706
N. D. R.
Amount paid at day of sale
Purchaser agrees to forward Insurance Policy to
State Land Department by
Grand Forks
Grand Forks
Interest
from
to
Expense conducting sale, advertising, etc
TOTAL
Description of Land SE¼
SECTION 36 TOWNSHIP 150 RANGE 52
STATE LAND DEPARTMENT AUCTIONEER
PURCHASER:
Signed
Signed

9. *Dad: The Cottonwood*
   Photo circa 1920, twigs, crate on linen
   matted with land sale document
   17" X 23"

The moon rises now white and round on a warm September evening, washes the leaves
                of the cottonwoods by the coulee

clean in silvery moonlight. All seasons come together as they do in dreams:
              I give them back to Mother, laced

with songs she gave me; songs about the garden where we walked, I listen
                with her for Jesus as he passes in rustling grass.

Byrd bore a roan colt they never named,
called him, Colt; grew up
to be the biggest horse in the county.
"Good for nothing,"
Dad said, "never once got him in harness."

The Fourth

A Prairie Hymn (2000–   )

I dreamed a long ship far from shore, shrouded in mist, silent like a ghost-ship.

—Daybook

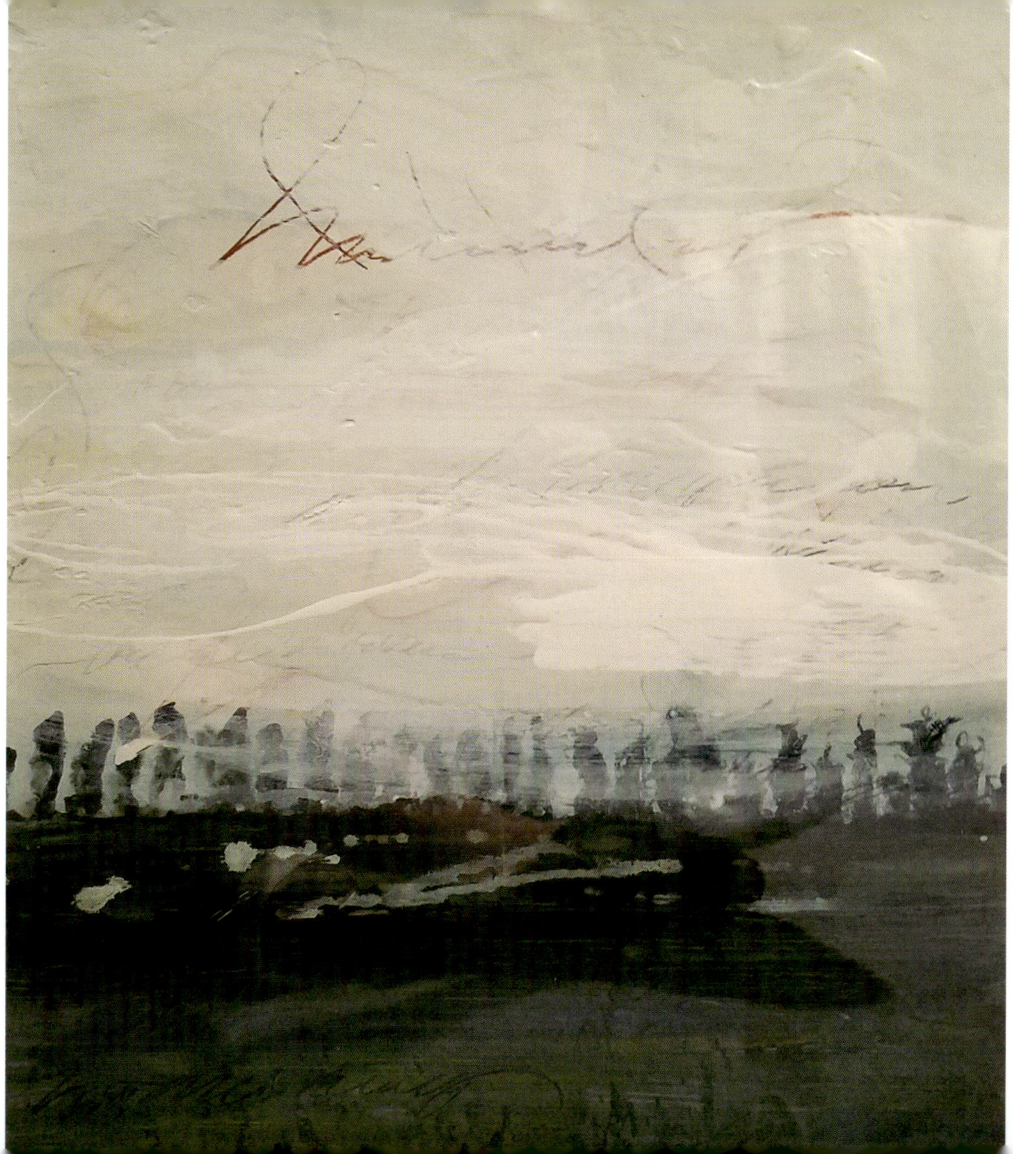

10. *This Land-Ocean*
    Acrylic, color pencil, graphite on board
    20" X 16"

Mother of water,

    I smell the ocean, taste the salt and ask for more. Hungry as a tongue first time
        at breast, I'm tossed back breathless,

    ride, grazing the salty wind through waves and foam. Oh yes, the foam, rash saliva
        of the ocean, white bubbling froth

    come from the deep green, moving out like lava burned to ashes. Mother of water,
        help me break this flat plain;

    let trees rise like spears, and grain elevators be harpoons. Sail with me, raise our mast,
        let it be like the canvas hung

    on a gray-weathered barn; let it lead us past these vacant farms, roofs that sag, walls
        shot full of holes; birds fly in

    and out like folded paper through broken windows. Grandmother, help me rescue
        ships wrecked on this ocean,

        keep us from tumbling; don't let us sink under a great wave.

The century rolls backward, forward; the poster beside the road reminds me:
DAKOTA WINDS, restaurant closed.

Fancy pick-ups whizz past, license plates with buffalo and stalks of wheat.
The man in a cap, his arm crooked

out the window seems to shout, HERE I AM on mailboxes painted with ducks
and flowers, posted on wheels

or welded links that mark farm driveways. *Hanson, Nelson*, in black or red, bold
letters like names in granite, saved

in the cemetery beside the road, white chain link fence.

I open my throat, my tongue sinuous as the rhythm of a track, up, down, back again;
                free at last of secrets; my mind

spins words, wheel to spindle, threads that catch and mend, curl wool from my head.
                The sum of my thought now

is these fields, woven with trees and coulees; my brain rushes like water after the thaw,
                tells what I see. I thunder off

with a lover I don't see on a horse; words fall behind me, words of truth that will stay
                long after I'm gone; will stay

like stones that mark our graves. My horse and I leap over ditches; we span the land
                like railroad tracks, barbed wire fences.

We are summer fallow, sunflower heads bent in rows; we are the willow branch in wind,
                my voice, leaf-like, opens on a stem,

spreads veins. I sing for miles and miles of grass; silvery blades reflect the land that
                gleamed for Grandmother, gleams now

        in the sun, brome and bluestem that sway like a waltz on the horizon.

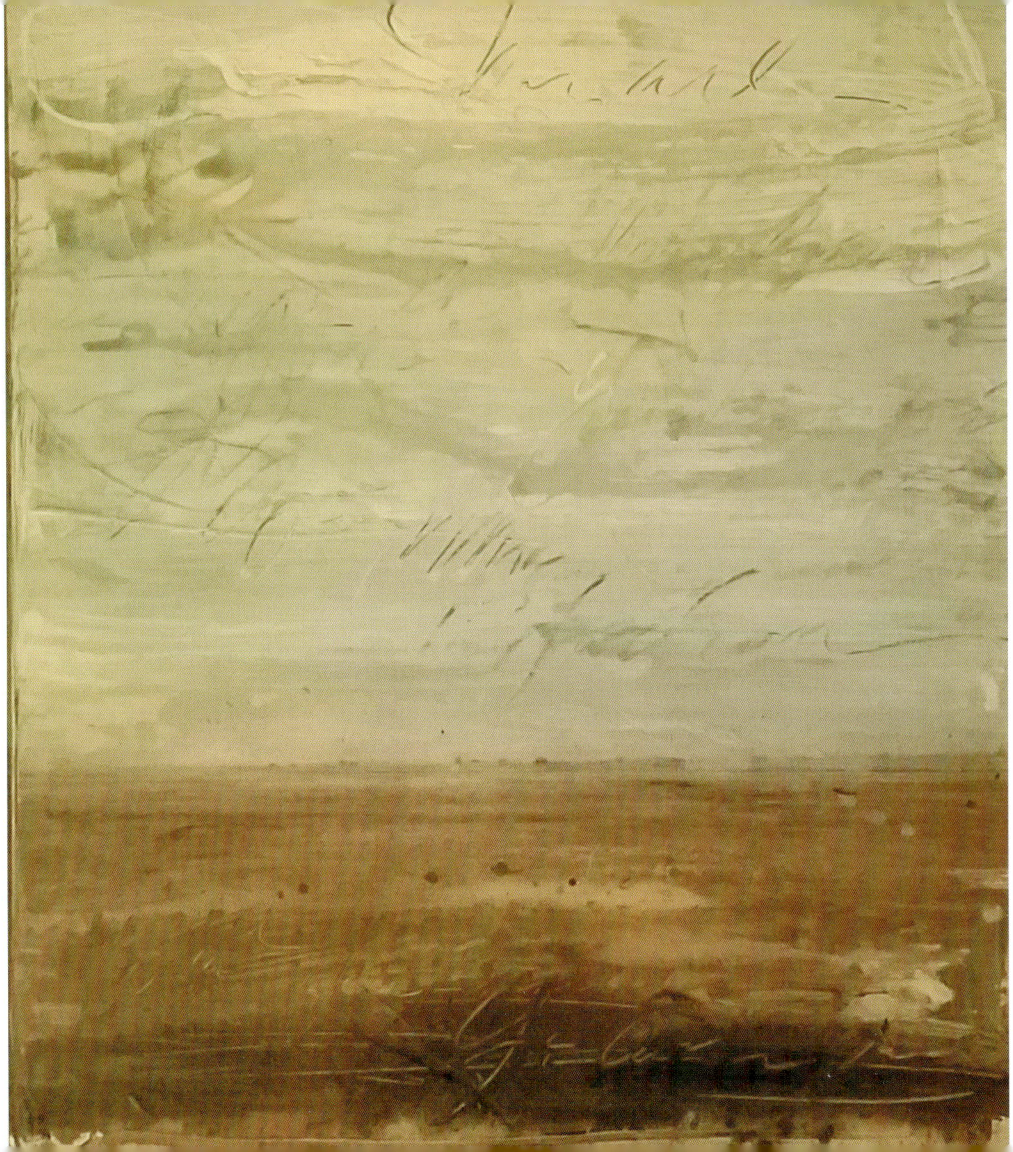

11. *The Land in Autumn*
    Acrylic on board
    20" X 16"

Pulled by wind and water, my horse and I ride as wind whistles around stones;
                a hundred years of graves that blend

the millennium. I'm coming home as if my life depended on grass, that long line
                that waves against the sky like the North Sea.

I'm at home with wind and sky; I breathe a misty seacoast. We ride the sweep
                of a tail, the mane from a neck, fierce as waves

that cross an ocean; words carry me and make me free. The threshing machine
                on a knoll, a tyrannosaurus rex of wheat:

bundles shucked, pitched; furrows plowed, land worked row by row, land marked
                with shacks, and in the window of one,

                the lamp Grandmother lit for strangers.

I have a horse now brave as Greyfell,
a horse strong and white; a horse to ride through flames—
a horse that flies at touch of the bridle.

Mother, at last I'm leaving your womb. I leave you standing on the doorstep,
your apron strings untying in the wind.

Leave you, your white handkerchief lace-edged that waves good-bye, a pinky
finger curled as if from your cup.

My horse and I pass through lips of grass that ripple up, down my spine; one
long pulse of earth drives me

to do this thing. I'm hungry as a tongue at breast, cheeks knowing only pull,
suck, suck, sucking. I come home,

head-first, home to gravel pits and hay bales set in stacks, I ride like the wind:
no desire but this: Live.

Live.

Live.

The bride in my dream, veiled, covered with white mesh, satin fabric and lace,
                stood at the mouth of a cave, bleeding

underneath. I watched her scrub as if to wash away all bloody trace; then she
                      went out to meet the groom, handsome in his suit.

When she looked at him and saw that mound, all big and swollen in his trousers,
                  she felt a stirring in her groin.

Jesus, Jesus, old women screamed,
called out their passion, their misery, from the church pew:
revival meetings spring and fall.
Come Lord make us pure.

In the dream, the horse lowered his great head.
I touched his ears, the soft flesh of
his nose, the slick hair
on his face;
I stroked his long neck muscle, then turned
and mounted him.

I ride to the river, my skin slippery as a fish; my spine grazes lips of grass, blades
yellow as spring shine under ice.

Washed in the blood of my mother, all the mothers before us, I'm hungry as
a tongue first time at breast.

Shaping new words, I say my name, its sound my own like it was when Mother
read it in that story, knew it was for me.

Let my name enter, letter by letter, let it heal me,
Mother, the name you gave me:

M-a-d-e-l-y-n-e.

M is easy like a church,
a the sprouted potato,
d a tire leaning against a tree;
e an apple half-eaten;
l merely a straight line;
y a fork in the road and *n* half an m;

The final e already forgotten when I learned
to spell my name,
seated on the hired man's lap:

Madelyn

I go back to grass and flowers, the lane framed by lilacs, and step barefoot through
                    mud puddles; hurry down the road

nubbed with gravel. Run to the little girl at the edge of the pasture; barbed wire
                    lifted, shoed low, I climb between.

Step into the orchard that blooms and grows like big sisters—women bear fruit.
                    Like Mother we gather plums
                            we tie in our aprons.

Mother wanders now in dreams, those she told me: she tries to find her house;
                        she enters forests, parts vines,

pulls thorns from her fingers, but she cannot reach the house. Always there is music,
                        someone singing close behind her.

One night she woke, hearing the baritone she dreamed; rose from bed, opened
                        cupboards, closets, tried to find him;

but he was nowhere. Other times, chased by white horses, she ran through tunnels,
                        heard hooves thundering,

and she looked for the stairs. Mother, Mother, please let the horses overtake you.

Roses spring up from white ashes along the shore of the coulee. My daughters
    emerge, flesh shiny like at birth;

water pours from inside me and they open like roses, dewy-fresh. They come
    to me and I hold them, clean

from the heart, and I wrap them with wet leaves. Suddenly, the wind rises the way
    a note becomes a waltz, that perfect

moment in a song when we give ourselves to love, when we know only the throb
    of notes, the beat, do not want to be

anywhere else; locked like lips in that first kiss, that wild, wild longing to open wide,
    stop time and fill it; we're caught

like that time in the moonlight, clouds passed, a gauze over the moon as the storm
    moved in from the west. The wind

rose and in the madness of branches, the old elm, leaves like hair blown, drawn into
    a knot as if from the face of a woman,

I danced out the storm with abandon, danced there on the lawn like an ocean
pulled under the moon; my feet

planted firmly in the earth, I had no fear of falling, all those stones under my feet
grown into rocks.

I take the voice of my father, heard once in a dream; he joined me in church,
                knelt beside me at the altar, his voice

rich, full like organ notes, tones held in that dream as if he had endless breath.
                I hear him again for my daughters,

for my sisters, for myself; we cry for ghosts we carry, cry for our sins, cry for
                our children. We blamed our mothers,

our sisters, ourselves. Horse, oh horse, all blame gone now, come carry me
                and carry my daughters. We are our mothers,

all the mothers come down from the shelf; we are all sisters, all daughters; we
                sing stories like hymns we pass on

to our children; stories to last as long as the sun, stories that cry for ghosts we
                carried; stories of horses that rescued us,

that saved us; horses that betrayed us. I cry for my sins, the sins of my mother,
                and those of my daughters, none of them

their own. I cry for the stones that have fallen at our feet. We no longer please the world; we are no longer horseless.

God change our blame to balm.

Let this month's moon be the moon
that will hold me, lift me up; let it carry me
like the hoof-beat of a horse.

In last night's dream, the lawn brilliant green, the way it looks just after rain,
                I said aloud, *This day looks like horses*—

and knew the day was glorious like winning a race. Hooves galloped around
                the grove, trees aflame, hooves

digging one plowed field to another; horses painted against the sky, glowing red
                and orange; horses running like bass notes

drumming. They break the glass, the dreams of a prince shattered. Horse, oh
                horse, warm my empty womb.

wooden cart on skids
to a wildly running
that late winter
rollin like
I chose to st
ling like a dirt clump
chose to stay with the
the outcome

12. *The Runaway*
    Drawing, photo collages, grasses, acrylic paint on canvas

Horse, oh horse,

    ride with us, ride with Mali, *bestemor*; rush us like water across the land that runs
        east to west, all its darkness coming clean.

Ride with Randi,

    oldemor; ride with her where the ice breaks into water, where it opens our faces,
        then closes them, like waves taking, letting go.

Ride with us,

    north and further, ride us like moths toward light. All the names we know
        move in and out our heads; names that sing a long line.

Ride with our daughters,

    and sing those names like the chimes outside my window; sing the ring of
        youth, those fleshy melodies rich as this land

        woven with coulees, wild flowers, and long grass.

Ride with us, *Mormor,* and *Mora mi,*

                                       ride with fire and energy, more dazzling than the sun.

Ride for our stories spoken, stories we carry; ride for the music in our minds, our hearts.

                         Horse, oh horse, free our tongues; ride us home.

Postlude

*That ship is gone,
but the sound of deep water
stays with me.*

Glossary

bestemor	grandmother
drukna i mølledam	drowned in the millstream
flornes	the village below Meråker. Mali boarded the train that took her to the fjord, the ocean and the steamship
fossen	waterfalls
four in a boat	a circle game intended for couples, play while singing; entertainment after an event at the schoolhouse
hund	dog
Hurtigruta	cruise boat off the western coast of Norway
Jeg leva i håpet som katta i skapet	I live in hope like the cat in the empty cupboard.
kjøtttboller	meatballs
kuer	cows
Lapland	the region where the Sámi, the indigenous people of Northern Europe, live. As with other contested lands taken from minority indigenous groups by majority groups, "Lapland" is a contested term not used today. Sámpi or Sámiland is preferred.
lefse	a potato and flour dough rolled thin and baked on a griddle, characterized by brown spots.
lutefisk	cod fish soaked in lye, a method of preserving fish used by Norwegian immigrants

Meråker	a landlocked municipality located in southern Nord-Trondelag county, not far from the Swedish border to the East.
mora mi	my mother
mormor	maternal grandmother
nedre	lower, in reference to a land location
oldemor	great-grandmother
ost	butter
Poison	running games played outdoors at recess by children attending country school
Pom, Pom, Pullaway	running games played outdoors at recess by children attending country school
posten	post office
potetklubb	potato dumplings
seter	a small mountain cabin used in summer for tending goats and cows
smør	cheese
Sonfossen	a land area in Norway
Stjørdalen	Lutheran church built in 1882, Grand Forks County, Union township, bordering Holmes general store at the edge of the German community. The church, vacated in the 1990s. Dismantled and torn down after the turn of the century, the bell is preserved in the gate to the well cared-for cemetery.
stoneboat	a simple flat board surface on skids for hauling stones; in this case, corn shucks
sur jord	sour land, dry soil mixed with stones
Trønder	person from northern Norway, near Trondhjem
vestre	west

About the Author

Madelyne Camrud was born and raised on a farm in North Dakota. She currently lives in Grand Forks, her home for more than sixty years. She received degrees from the University of North Dakota in Visual Arts and English in 1988, and a master's degree in English in 1990. New Rivers Press has published two collections of her poems: *This House Is Filled with Cracks* (Minnesota Voices Project Winner 1994) and *Oddly Beautiful*, 2013. Her chapbook, *The Light We Go After*, Dacotah Territory Press, came out in 2006. Her poems have appeared in publications such as *Painted Bride Quarterly, Soundings East, Water~Stone Review*, and *New Millennium Writings* among others. Several of her poems were chosen for Garrison Keillor's *Writer's Almanac*. Camrud has attended multiple retreats, workshops, and conferences over the years, and she credits the University of North Dakota Writers Conference for her commitment to becoming a poet. She was named an Associate Poet Laureate for North Dakota in 2005. Her next collection, *On the Way to Moon Island*, is nearing completion.